STANLEY
KUBRICK

STANLEY
KUBRICK
A BIOGRAPHY

John Baxter

Carroll & Graf Publishers, Inc.
New York

First Carroll & Graf edition 1997

Carroll & Graf Publishers, Inc.
19 West 21st Street
New York, NY 10010

Library of Congress Cataloging-in-Publication Data
Baxter, John, 1939–
Stanley Kubrick : a biography / John Baxter. —
1st Carroll & Graf Ed.
p. cm.
ISBN 0-7867-0485-3 (pbk.)
1. Kubrick, Stanley. 2. Motion picture producers and directors—
United States— Biography.   I. Title.
PN1998.3.K83B35   1997
791.43'0233'092—dc21
[B]   97-19738
                                         CIP

Manufactured in the United States of America

For Marie-Dominique and Louise

–there is an importance of beauty
Which can't be accounted for by there and then–

BERNARD SPENCER, 'Part of Plenty'

Contents

Illustrations

Russian Amabassador DeSadesky (Peter Bull) and President Merkin
Muffley (Peter Sellers) in the deleted pie-fight sequence. (*Estate of Arthur
Fellig; Weegee the Famous/International Center for Photography, New
York*)

Kubrick directs Sellers as the sinister Dr Strangelove. (*British Film
Institute*)

Frank Poole (Gary Lockwood) and Dave Bowman (Keir Dullea) in *2001: A
Space Odyssey*. (*Author's collection*)

Poole jogs round the living quarters of the *Discovery*.
Kubrick shooting the sequence. (*Author's collection*)

The exterior of the $750,000 Vickers-Armstrong centrifuge. (*Andrew
Birkin*)

Heywood Floyd and his party descend into the excavation in Tycho where
the monolith was unearthed. (*Author's collection*)

Marlon Brando with Karl Malden in *One-Eyed Jacks*, which Kubrick
prepared but Brando directed. (*Author's collection*)

Kubrick lining up the shot in which Alex (Malcolm McDowell) attacks the
Cat Lady in *A Clockwork Orange*. (*British Film Institute*)

Mrs Alexander (Adrienne Corri) about to be raped by Alex and his *droogs*
while Kubrick operates the camera. (*British Film Institute*)

Kubrick on the prison set with Michael Bryant and Malcolm McDowell.
(*British Film Institute*)

Kubrick on the prison chapel set. (*British Film Institute*)

One of Kubrick's cost-cutting technical innovations: a wheelchair adapted
into a camera platform. (*British Film Institute*)

Kubrick directs *Barry Lyndon*. (*Author's collection*)

Marisa Berenson as Lady Lyndon. (*British Film Institute*)

Lady Lyndon and her chaplain, the Reverend Runt (Murray Melvin), in
one of the gaming-room scenes which Kubrick insisted be shot by candle-
light. (*British Film Institute*)

Kubrick on the set of *The Shining*. (*British Film Institute*)

Kubrick with director of photography John Alcott. (*British Film Institute*)

Lee Ermey as Sergeant Hartman rages at the recruits in *Full Metal Jacket*.
(*British Film Institute*)

The death of Cowboy (Arliss Howard), from *Full Metal Jacket*. (*British
Film Institute*)

Acknowledgements

Jean-Pierre Thierry suggested this book. He thought Stanley Kubrick was an obvious subject, given the way I never stopped talking about *The Shining* and *Full Metal Jacket*. Once he brought it up, Kubrick did seem an obvious subject for a biography, but an impossible one. Surely Kubrick's passion for privacy, frequently and powerfully expressed, would be respected by his friends and colleagues. A chance conversation with his brother-in-law and business manager Jan Harlan at a party seemed to confirm this view. Nobody was going to talk to me about Stanley.

Thus is the bright hue of resolution sicklied o'er with the pale cast of thought. Because researching this book was less a question of seeking out material than of restraining the flow. Ten-minute interviews turned into three- and four-hour monologues during which people wept and laughed – well, mostly wept, really – as they recounted what it had been like to work with Kubrick. Halfway down the steps, they would turn back to say, 'Listen, did I tell you about the time...?'

Everyone, it seems, has a Kubrick story, but my particular gratitude goes to the following who offered theirs, and made my work so illuminating and pleasurable.

Ken Adam, Brian Aldiss, Richard Anderson, Professor Bob Anderson, Jean-Claude Barsacq, Louis Begley, Andrew Birkin, Bernard Cohn, Adrienne Corri, Roger de Vito, Jules Feiffer, Jerry Goldsmith, Curtis Harrington, James B. Harris, Michael Herr, Tana Hoban, William Hootkins, Diane Johnson, Allen Jones, Alan Kaufman, Gavin Lambert, Scott Martin at Shepperton Studios, the late James Mason, John G. Morris, Jerry and Janice Pam, David Perry, Sir David Puttnam, Shane Rimmer, the late Bob Shaw, Kerry Shale, Alexander Singer, David Slavitt, Gordon Stainforth, Fred Stettner, Erika Stoll, Bertrand Tavernier, Walter Trueman, Lisa Tuttle, David Vaughan and Paul Vaughan, John Ward, Derek Ware, John Whitwell and William Read Woodfield.

Denise Bethel directed me to the International Center for Photography in New York, the curator of which, Miles Barth, made available Weegee's 'lost' stills from *Dr Strangelove*. Charles Silver, Ron Magliozzi and Mary Corliss of the Museum of Modern Art, New York, were their customary courteous and helpful selves. Michael Neal made available his limitless knowledge of erotica by elucidating the more obscure *couloirs* of *Lolita* and the Olympia Press. The National Film Theatre, London, kindly supplied a tape of Paul Mazursky's lecture there. Paolo Cherchi Usai and his staff at George Eastman House in Rochester NY made available both their rare copy of *Fear and Desire* and their documentation on the film's distribution. Without the help of the American Chess Federation and Chess Foundation, I would never have found Alan Kaufman and learned of Kubrick's early life in New York.

Arvad Kompanetz drove me around the Bronx in a blizzard on the track of Kubrick's childhood haunts. June Cullen of Griffith University in Queensland directed me to Kevin Rockett in Dublin and Commandant Peter Young of Ireland's National Military Archive, both of whom illuminated the politics surrounding the production of *Barry Lyndon*. Bill Warren lent books, arranged interviews and otherwise helped with research. Professor Matthew Bernstein drew my attention to a number of articles on Dalton Trumbo and his contribution to *Spartacus*. The BBC's Mark Burman suggested additional sources from his own programme research. Adrian Turner supplied unpublished interviews, letters and clippings, and with his wife Andrea took me on a tour of Childwick Bury and Kubrick country. Adrian also read the manuscript and made a number of insightful suggestions for improving it, as did David Stratton, Bill Warren, Michael Ciment and David Thompson.

David Thompson also provided much valuable documentation, including copies of the complete versions of *The Shining*, *Making The Shining* and *Killer's Kiss*, and of Kubrick's early documentaries, and John Brosnan gave access to a number of rare interviews as well as to material recorded for his books *Future Tense*, *Movie Magic* and *The Primal Screen*. Lee Hill made available sections of his forthcoming biography of Terry Southern, and was unstinting in clarifying the thorny relationship between Southern and Kubrick. Patrick McGilligan also kindly allowed me to quote from Lee's interview with Southern in a forthcoming edition of his *Backstory* series. Weidenfeld & Nicolson gave me permission to quote passages from Vladimir Nabokov's *Lolita*.

In Paris, Kristi Jaas helped with document research and interviews, and Tuki Jancquel with translations. Jackie and Patrick Morreau never complained when their home was turned into a combined office, answering service and hospitality suite. Brian Troath tracked down the rarest books, and without Mary Troath's indefatigable research, this book would have been greatly diminished. Richard Johnson proved once again the most supportive and diplomatic of editors. To all of these people and to the others who helped, not least my wife Marie-Dominique, my profound gratitude.

John Baxter
Paris, 1997